First World War
and Army of Occupation
War Diary
France, Belgium and Germany

59 DIVISION
176 Infantry Brigade
South Staffordshire Regiment
2/5th (T.F.) Battalion
4 January 1916 - 19 February 1916

WO95/3021/6

The Naval & Military Press Ltd
www.nmarchive.com
Published in association with The National Archives

Published by

The Naval & Military Press Ltd

Unit 10 Ridgewood Industrial Park,

Uckfield, East Sussex,

TN22 5QE England

Tel: +44 (0) 1825 749494

www.naval-military-press.com

www.nmarchive.com

This diary has been reprinted in facsimile from the original. Any imperfections are inevitably reproduced and the quality may fall short of modern type and cartographic standards.

© **Crown Copyright**
Images reproduced by permission of The National Archives, London, England, 2015.

Contents

Document type	Place/Title	Date From	Date To
Heading	WO95/3021/6		
Heading	War Diary of 2/5th Battalion South Staffordshire Regt For January 1916 (Volume 1)		
War Diary	St Albans	04/01/1916	31/01/1916
Miscellaneous	Appendix		
Miscellaneous	A Form Messages And Signals		
Miscellaneous	Recd /8.25 Jan		
Miscellaneous	A Form Messages And Signals		
Miscellaneous	Recd 7.25		
Miscellaneous	A Form Messages And Signals		
Heading	War Diary of 2/5th Battalion South Staffordshire Regiment From February 1st 1916 To February 29th 1916 (Volume II)		
War Diary	St Albans	02/02/1916	19/02/1916

wdqb30216

Confidential

— War Diary —

of

2/5th Battalion South Staffordshire Regt.

— for —

— January 1916. —

(Volume I)

Army Form C. 2118.

WAR DIARY
or
INTELLIGENCE SUMMARY.
(Erase heading not required.)

Instructions regarding War Diaries and Intelligence Summaries are contained in F. S. Regs., Part II. and the Staff Manual respectively. Title pages will be prepared in manuscript.

Hour, Date, Place	Summary of Events and Information	Remarks and References to Appendices
ST ALBANS		
January 4th 1916	Lieutenant (Temporary Captain) HAROLD E. McGOWAN transferred to 2/5 Batt: S.S. Regt from 2/5 Batt: N.S. Regt.	appx
January 13th 1916	59th North Mid Division came to be directly under the Command of G.O.C. in C. Central Force & come under the Command of G.O.C. 3rd Army.	Div'l Order 77/13/1/16 appx appx appx
January 22nd 1916	Arrival of 17 Derby Recruits from WALSALL	
January 23rd 1916	Arrival of 30 Derby Recruits from WALSALL	
January 26th 1916	Arrival of 19 Derby Recruits from WALSALL	
January 27th 1916	Establishment Numbers of Corporals increased by 2 per Company. Paid Lance Corporals correspondingly reduced by 8.-	W.O. letter No 20/Inf/600. (SD2.AC1. 19th Jan 1916. appx
January 27th 1916	Arrival of 30 Derby Recruits from WALSALL	appx
January 28th 1916	Arrival of 21 Derby Recruits from WALSALL	appx
January 29th 1916	Arrival of 38 Derby Recruits from WALSALL	appx
January 31st 1916	Arrival of 6 Derby Recruits from WALSALL	appx
January 31st 1916	Notification of Zepplins raid on Eastern Counties.	Appendices Nos 1, 2, 3, 4. appx

W. O. Lyrmnn S. Col
Commanding 2/5 South Staffs.

Appendix

No	Subject	Issuing Authority
1.	Zepplin Raid	176th Infantry Brigade
2.	do.	do.
3.	do	do.
4.	do	do.

"A" Form.   Army Form C. 2121.
MESSAGES AND SIGNALS.

TO: 7Bn S Staffs R

Day of Month: 31st

Firing parties will be warned to turn out on receiving further orders; pending which orders they will not be turned out.

From: B HQ
Time: 7.45 pm

176 Inf Bde

Rec'd 8.25 am

"A" Form.
Army Form C. 2121.

MESSAGES AND SIGNALS.

No. of Message _____

Prefix _____ Code _____ m.	Words	Charge	This message is on a/c of:	Recd. at _____ m.
Office of Origin and Service Instructions	Sent			Date _____
_____	At _____ m.		_____ Service.	From _____
_____	To _____			By _____
_____	By _____		(Signature of "Franking Officer.")	

TO { O.C. 2/5th S. Staffs R

| Sender's Number. | Day of Month. | In reply to Number | | AAA |
| * | 31/1/16 | | | |

The	following	Telephone	message	just
received	from	Divisional	Headquarters.	
3	Zeppelins	on	the	way
to	London	working	from	Cambridge
all	traffic	stopped	on	G.E.
line.	aaa.	Please	act	in
accordance	with	air	Raid	orders
at	once.	Firing	parties	will
be	detailed	aaa		①

From Bde Headquarters
Place
Time 6.35 pm 7.5 pm

The above may be forwarded as now corrected. (Z)

Censor. Colonel Capt
176th Infantry Bde

Signature of Addressor or person authorised to telegraph in his name.

* This line should be erased if not required.

Recd. 7.25.

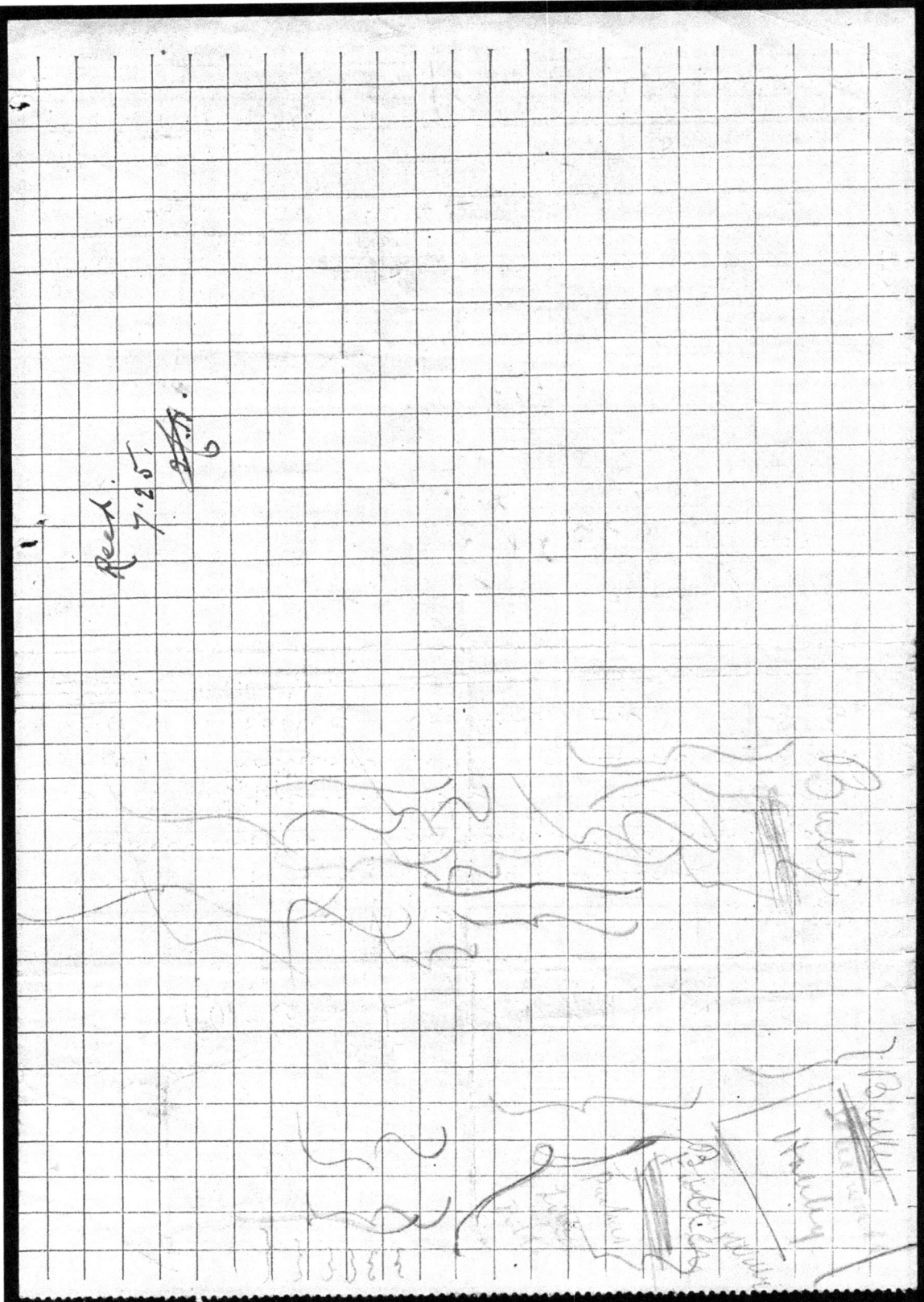

"A" Form.   Army Form C. 2121.
MESSAGES AND SIGNALS.

TO: 7th Staffs R

Day of Month: 31st

Firing parties are to be called in but to be prepared to turn out if required

(4)

Recd 10.10 pm

From: B 18 R
Time: 9.30 pm

C. O. Caun... Capt.

"A" Form. Army Form C. 2121.
MESSAGES AND SIGNALS. No. of Message............

TO	O6 2/5 S Staff R		
Sender's Number.	Day of Month. 31/1/16	In reply to Number	A A A

The following message has been received from Divisional Headquarters

2 Zeppelins at BROXBOURNE in Herts at 7.30pm aaa Firing Parties will turn out.

(3)

From Bde H.Q.
Place
Time 8 15 pm

Confidential

War Diary

of

2/5th Battalion South Staffordshire Regiment

from February 1st 1916 to February 29th 1916

(Volume II)

2/5th Battalion South Staffordshire Regt.

WAR DIARY or **INTELLIGENCE SUMMARY.**

Army Form C. 2118.

(Erase heading not required.)

Hour, Date, Place	Summary of Events and Information	Remarks and references to Appendices
ST ALBANS		
February 2nd 1916	Arrival of 9 Derby Recruits from WALSALL	appx
February 2nd 1916	Death of No. 8655 Private SWINNERTON W at BRICKET HOUSE Hospital (Gangrene of lungs after Pneumonia)	appx
February 4th 1916	65 h.O. ors & men transferred to 28th Provisional Battalion at NEWCASTLE ON TYNE.	appx
February 4th 1916	Arrival of 14 Derby Recruits from WALSALL	appx
February 5th 1916	Arrival of 15 Derby Recruits from WALSALL	appx
February 8th 1916	Arrival of 10 Derby Recruits from WALSALL	appx
February 10th 1916	Arrival of 9 Derby Recruits from WALSALL	appx
February 11th 1916	Arrival of 8 Derby Recruits from WALSALL	appx
February 12th 1916	Arrival of 34 Derby Recruits from WALSALL	appx
February 14th 1916	Arrival of 13 Derby Recruits from WALSALL	appx
February 15th 1916	Arrival of 6 Derby Recruits from WALSALL	appx
	Major Colonel R N R READE. O.C. having however taken up another appointment handed over the Command of the Division. Major General A.E. SANDBACH. C.B. D.S.O. having been appointed to Command the Division taken over the Command as from this date inclusive (Div Orders Feb 14/1916.	appx

2/5th Battalion South Staffordshire Regt.

WAR DIARY
or
INTELLIGENCE SUMMARY.

Army Form C. 2118.

(Erase heading not required.)

Hour, Date, Place	Summary of Events and Information	Remarks and references to Appendices
ST ALBANS. February 16th 1916	Arrival of 29 Duty Recruits from WALSALL	
February 17th 1916	Arrival of 19 Duty Recruits from WALSALL. Colonel R L CARLTON. D.S.O. (G.S.O. I. North Midd Divn) having been appointed to command the 176th Infantry Brigade took over command of the Brigade from Feb 16/16. Colonel J A CHANDOS, POLE-FELL vacated the command + is struck off the strength of 59th Division accordingly	Divisional Order No 289. 16/2/16
February 18th 1916	Arrival of 13 Duty Recruits from WALSALL	
February 19th 1916	Arrival of 40 Duty Recruits from WALSALL	

R.S. Symmonds Lt Col.
Comdg 2/5 Batt South Staff Regt.